BITTEN BY A RATTLESNAKE

Sue Hamilton

Visit us at
WWW.ABDOPUBLISHING.COM

Published by ABDO Publishing Company, 8000 West 78th Street, Suite 310, Edina, MN 55439. Copyright ©2010 by Abdo Consulting Group, Inc. International copyrights reserved in all countries. No part of this book may be reproduced in any form without written permission from the publisher. ABDO & Daughters™ is a trademark and logo of ABDO Publishing Company.

Printed in the United States of America, North Mankato, Minnesota
112009
012010

♻ PRINTED ON RECYCLED PAPER

Editor & Cover Design: John Hamilton
Graphic Design: Sue Hamilton
Cover Photo: Getty Images
Interior Photos and Illustrations: AP Images, p. 4, 20, 23, 32; Coghlan's, p. 29; Discovery Channel, p. 19, 21; FotoSearch, p. 12; Getty Images, p. 6, 27, 29; iStockphoto, p. 26; National Geographic, p. 8, 13, 14, 28; Peter Arnold, p. 3, 5, 7, 15, 25; Photo Researchers, p. 1, 9, 10, 11, 12, 16, 17; Visuals Unlimited, p. 18.

Library of Congress Cataloging-in-Publication Data

Hamilton, Sue L., 1959-
  Bitten by a rattlesnake / Sue Hamilton.
    p. cm. -- (Close encounters of the wild kind)
  Includes index.
  ISBN 978-1-60453-930-1
  1. Snake attacks--Juvenile literature. 2. Rattlesnakes--Venom--Juvenile literature. 3. Rattlesnakes--Venom--Physiological effect--Juvenile literature. I. Title.
  QL666.O69H36 2010
  597.96'38--dc22
                    2009045423

CONTENTS

DEATH RATTLE

The dry rattling sound is unmistakable. People instinctively know that a rattlesnake's warning noise means danger, and sometimes death. There are 26 species of rattlesnakes, and nature has provided these reptiles with the senses and skills to hunt and protect themselves. Large fangs, and venom lethal enough to kill a human, make these predators both frightening and impressive.

In reality, only about 8,000 snakebites occur in the United States each year. Of these, fewer than 10 people die from the venom. About 1/4 of the bites are "dry," which means no venom is injected. You are nine times more likely to die from being struck by lightning than to die from a venomous snakebite.

However, people who do not receive immediate medical attention will see the venom begin to digest their flesh. Survivors may be left with disfiguring reminders of what venom can do when they are bitten by a rattlesnake.

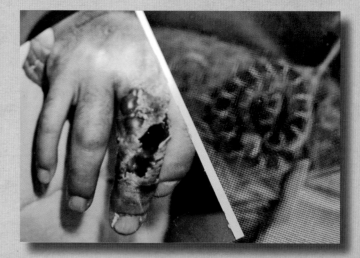

Right: Even people who are snake experts may sometimes be bitten. This photo shows the snake-bitten hand of Russ Johnson, president of the Phoenix Herpetological Society, a group that studies reptiles and amphibians.
Facing page: A western diamondback rattlesnake displays its rattle-like tail.

RATTLESNAKE SENSES

Rattlesnakes eat small mammals, birds, lizards, and even other snakes. They provide a vital service in controlling pest populations. Their senses are designed to quickly and efficiently find, kill, and eat their prey.

Rattlesnakes' lidless eyes can see movement about 40 feet (12 m) away. As members of the pit viper family, rattlesnakes also have loreal pits. These pits are heat sensors that allow the snakes to locate warm-blooded animals simply by their body heat. The loreal pits are located on either side of a rattlesnake's face, between its eyes and nostrils.

Loreal Pit

Above: Rattlesnakes have loreal pits on either side of their face that act as heat sensors. These pits allow rattlers to locate warm-blooded animals simply by their body heat.

Above: A western diamondback rattlesnake eats a wood rat.

> "A rattlesnake that doesn't bite teaches you nothing."
> —Jessamyn West, American Author

Snakes hear and smell using several senses. Their scales and bones are sensitive enough to detect air-to-ground vibrations, letting them feel their prey's footsteps or other movements. Rattlers have nostrils lined with olfactory (smelling) cells that allow them to detect odors, but they mainly use their tongues to smell.

When a rattlesnake's forked tongue flicks out, it picks up chemical molecules in the air and on the ground. When the tongue retracts back inside the mouth, the snake transfers the microscopic particles to the roof of its mouth, where a special sensory organ, called the Jacobson's organ, is located. It processes the chemical odors and sends the information to the snake's brain, which identifies the smells as food, enemy, or mate.

Above: A Baja California rattlesnake uses its tongue to pick up surrounding smells.

Rattlesnakes "hear" using their scales and bones to detect air-to-ground vibrations. This image shows a regular photo of a southern Pacific rattlesnake combined with a high resolution x-ray.

FANGS AND VENOM

attlers have hypodermic-like fangs. When a snake opens its mouth to strike, strong muscles untuck these hollow, needle-like tubes, moving them down to 90-degree angles. This vertical position allows the rattlesnake to stab the fangs deep into its victim. If a fang falls out or is caught in a victim, another fang comes in to replace it. Rattlesnake fangs are lost and replaced every month or so.

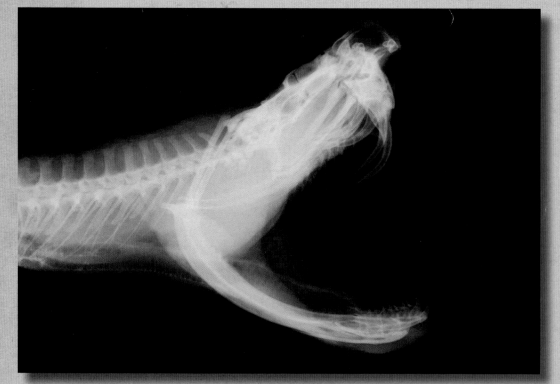

Above: An x-ray of an eastern diamondback rattlesnake, showing how the fangs drop down to 90-degree angles when the mouth is open.

Rattlesnake venom is a saliva-like fluid held in venom sacs behind a snake's cheeks. The venom is a hemotoxin. This means that as soon as it enters a body, it begins to break down and digest flesh. It may also keep blood from clotting, so a victim can't stop bleeding. Sometimes venom also affects muscle control. Victims may experience muscle twitches in their face, neck, and chest. They may begin gasping for breath.

Rattlesnake venom is strong because, as legless creatures, these snakes are not fast movers. However, their prey is usually quite speedy. Mice and birds would be long gone if a rattlesnake's venom didn't work quickly. But humans are much bigger. The effects of snake venom take several minutes. This helps give people time to get to a hospital and receive antivenin, the medication that stops the damage. But since shy rattlesnakes tend to live in remote areas, many people are bitten while hiking, camping, or hunting far from medical help. When victims can't get to a hospital quickly, they soon begin to feel the pain of a rattlesnake's venom.

Above: Rattlesnakes crawl at a top speed of 3 miles per hour (5 kph), while mice run at a speed of 8 mph (13 kph). A rattler's prey could get away if the venom didn't work fast.

"Baby rattlesnakes are *not* more 'deadly' than adults. However, they are poisonous and capable of biting from the moment of birth." —Southwestern Herpetologists Society

Above: A rattlesnake's venom is held in sacs behind a snake's cheeks.

WESTERN DIAMONDBACK

Arizona is home to 17 different species of rattlesnake, more than any other U.S. state. Rattlesnakes bite about 150 people in Arizona each year. Western diamondbacks account for many of these bites. Growing to a length of more than five feet (1.5 m), the diamondback's sheer size and large numbers have given it the distinction of causing the most serious and fatal snakebites of any North American reptile.

Managing Director Jude McNally, of the Arizona Poison & Drug Information Center, states, "Western diamondback is the most common snake that we find throughout Arizona, and actually grows to be the largest. If someone's been bitten by a western diamondback, the most important thing is to get to a health care facility as soon as possible." In 2008, an Arizona woman named Lian found out how important it is to get to a hospital quickly.

Above: Western diamondbacks grow to more than 5 feet (1.5 m) in length.

On August 27, 2008, a friend shot video while Lian worked in a garden in Tucson, Arizona. As she bent down to tend a plant, a four-foot (1.2-m) long western diamondback bit her on the knuckle of her left hand. Unlike most rattlesnake encounters, the diamondback did not give a warning rattle until after Lian was bitten.

With her hand beginning to swell and in great pain, Lian's friends rushed her to a local emergency room. Lian was admitted to intensive care, where she spent three days and was given more than 20 vials of antivenin. Her hand and armed swelled to more than double its normal size. "I look like Popeye," she remarked, referring to the large-armed cartoon character.

Lian survived and healed. It took a long time for the pain to stop, and she was left with her finger permanently bent. However, Lian was lucky because she was close to a hospital and received the proper antivenin.

Above: A person's finger five days after being bitten by a western diamondback. The venom causes almost immediate pain and swelling, and must be treated with antivenin.

"I feel like my hand is being eaten by ravenous ants."

—Lian, August 27, 2008, Tucson, Arizona

Above: A western diamondback rattlesnake strikes. Western diamondbacks are the most common snake in Arizona. The large number of diamondbacks, plus their large size, give them the distinction of causing the most serious and fatal snakebites of any North American reptile.

SOUTHERN PACIFIC

Southern Pacific rattlesnakes are found in southwestern California and Mexico's Baja California. Also called a western rattlesnake or black diamond rattlesnake, these snakes live in many areas, including prairies, grasslands, beaches, and pine-wooded mountains.

As people have moved into the snakes' territory, encounters have increased. "Southern Pacific rattlesnakes thrive where people prefer to live, so people encounter them relatively frequently," said Dr. Sean Bush, an emergency room doctor and snake researcher at Loma Linda University Medical Center in Loma Linda, California. Southern Pacific rattlesnakes account for the most number of bites of any type of rattlesnake in the Los Angeles and San Diego areas. One California man now knows this rattlesnake is much better left alone.

Above: A southern Pacific rattlesnake.

Pippin Graves had spent the day with friends at a California lake. On the drive home, Graves sat in back of a friend's pickup truck as they bumped along a rough backcountry road. Suddenly, the truck screeched to a halt. One of Graves' friends had spotted a southern Pacific rattlesnake at the side of the road, and wanted to bring it home. Graves, who had handled snakes before, grabbed the rattler and placed it in a plastic garbage bag. Then they continued their journey down the road.

During the bumpy ride, the bag with the rattler opened, and the snake wriggled out. Graves knocked on the back window and told his friend to stop the truck, then jumped out. The angry serpent slithered across the truck bed. Graves reached in and grabbed its tail, then slid his hand up behind the reptile's head. But the snake had enough room to twist around and strike Graves' right hand. "The snake didn't strike and let go. It kind of latched on. We actually had to pry his head... like pull him off," Graves said. Seeing spots of blood from the fangs, he knew he was in trouble.

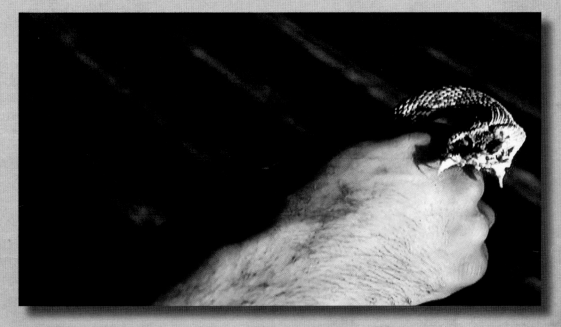

Above: The Discovery Channel's *I've Been Bitten* show demonstrates how the rattlesnake had enough room to twist around and bite Pippin Graves in the hand.

Above: A medical helicopter was used to quickly transport Pippin Graves to the hospital.

Help was a long ride away. His friends rushed him to a ranger station, but it was closed. They flagged down another driver, who had a cell phone and called 911. By this time, Graves' neck had swollen and he was having trouble breathing. Emergency medical technicians arrived in an ambulance. Graves was turning blue from lack of oxygen, and was confused and fighting his rescuers. They were able to get a breathing tube in him, but he needed additional medical care. A helicopter was called and Graves was flown to the Loma Linda University Medical Center.

When Graves finally reached the hospital, he was immediately given antivenin, but a lot of time had passed. The venom had spread, causing immense swelling on his entire upper body and cutting off the blood supply to his muscles. This severe reaction is called compartment syndrome. Surgeons treat it by performing a fasciotomy, using a scalpel to cleanly slice open different sections of the swollen tissue. Graves was sliced open in several places from his right hand all the way up his arm.

Graves survived the surgery. After a few days, skin grafts helped close the open wounds on his arm. Although he has some loss of movement, he still has partial use of his hand and arm. He is quick to say, "I feel lucky to be alive."

> # "The swelling was so intense that my arm would have just basically popped."
> —Pippin Graves, *I've Been Bitten*, Discovery Channel

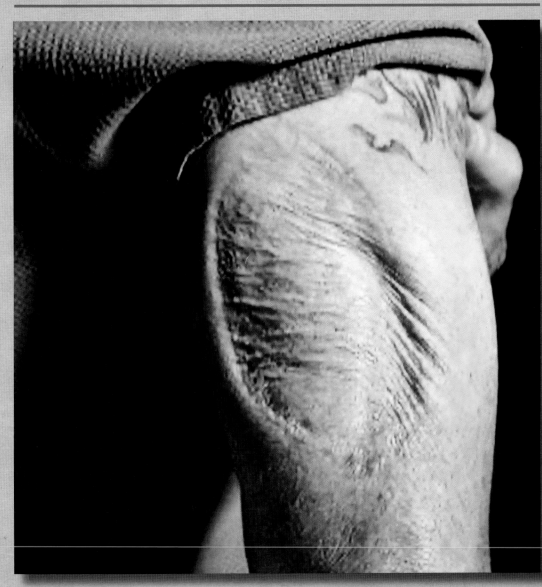

Above: A view of Pippin Graves' arm from his interview on the Discovery Channel's *I've Been Bitten* TV show. Graves had a severe reaction to the rattlesnake venom. His arm swelled to the point that surgery was required to relieve the fluid build-up. The scar shows how skin was grafted onto Graves' arm to close the wound created by the surgery.

EASTERN DIAMONDBACK

Eastern diamondback rattlesnakes are found from North Carolina to Florida to Louisiana. The aggressive snake does not like human contact. It usually lives in woods or coastal beaches. As the heaviest rattlesnake, it can weigh up to 10 pounds (4.5 kg). The big snake's fangs grow to nearly half an inch (1.3 cm) long. When an eastern diamondback strikes, its head moves at a speed of 175 miles per hour (282 kph).

An eastern diamondback's venom is both powerful and fast working. One bite has enough venom to kill six humans. This venom is a neurotoxin. It is particularly painful, and causes nearly immediate breathing problems. In 2006, a Florida police officer discovered the terrifying effects of an eastern diamondback's bite.

On November 24, 2006, Deputy Sheriff Brandon Parker of Hillsborough County, Florida, was off duty, hiking with a friend deep in a wooded area. Suddenly, an eastern diamondback reared up and bit the officer on the left leg. "After the bite I felt the burning sensation, my hands started tingling, my legs were tingling, and my face was tingling," Parker said.

He and his friend knew they had to get Parker back to civilization as soon as possible for antivenin. They immediately began walking out of the woods. "I thought that I would actually be able to walk slowly and calmly all the way to the truck," said Parker. But within nine minutes, the powerful venom began affecting his body and his brain. Parker collapsed. "I thought this might be it," the deputy sheriff said.

> "I can remember very distinctly, my hands and feet instantaneously started tingling. I knew that was a telltale sign that I was envenomated."
>
> —Brandon Parker, November 24, 2006, Ruskin, Florida

Left untreated, an eastern diamondback's bite is often fatal. But Parker, thinking of his family, survived. He was given antivenin and medical treatment. As a deputy sheriff, he remains the person to call if a rattlesnake is found in someone's house or yard. He is careful to wear protective gear and boots, and watches where he steps when he's hiking. "If it could happen to me, and I've been around snakes and handling snakes just about my whole life, it could happen to anyone," Parker says.

A snake wrangler catches an eastern diamondback rattlesnake. Their venom is a neurotoxin, which causes nearly immediate breathing problems for its victims.

DEAD RATTLER'S BITE

Most people are scared of rattlesnakes when the reptiles are alive and rattling. But a scientific study shows that people should also worry about recently killed snakes biting them. Bill Sloan of the Arizona Herpetological Association says, "There's a reflex action involved when you touch a snake's mouth. The fang is like a hypodermic needle. It's going to continue to work if you put your hand near it."

Justin Cluff of Queen Creek, Arizona, knows this is true. Cluff had picked up a dead Mojave rattlesnake, which his friend had recently shot. As Cluff held the reptile's head, a fang shot out and sank into the man's knuckle, injecting the 21-year-old with a full dose of venom. "The pain was terrible," said Cluff. Mojave rattlesnakes are known for their frequent strikes and long fangs.

Dr. Jeffrey Suchard and Dr. Frank LoVecchio, toxicologists from Phoenix, Arizona, conducted a study of Arizona rattlesnake victims. They discovered that over the course of 11 months, 5 of the 34 patients who had been admitted to a hospital for rattlesnake bites, nearly 15 percent, had been bitten after the snake was dead. Another study indicated that

rattlesnake heads could be dangerous 20 minutes to an hour after being removed from the snakes' bodies.

Cluff has a lasting reminder that a dead snake is still a dangerous snake. He ended up losing part of his right index finger to the dead snake's venom.

"That snake was really juiced up. He got me good."

—Justin Cluff, Queen Creek, Arizona, 1999

Above: A Mojave rattlesnake preparing to strike.

SURVIVING A BITE

Rattlesnakes bite people not for food—they know we're too big to eat—but to defend and protect themselves. Their venom acts quickly to stop their prey from getting away, and then begins digesting the animals from the inside. However, not all rattlesnakes release venom when they bite.

It's unknown if rattlesnakes can choose whether or not to shoot venom into their victims, but it's estimated that as much as 25 percent of the time, rattlers hit their victims with a dry bite. A dry bite is when no venom comes out. However, when venom is released, it is only a few minutes later that humans feel and see the burning and swelling that show they've been envenomated.

To avoid being bitten by a rattlesnake, be very aware of your surroundings when in rattler territory. Always watch where you are stepping and sitting. Wear hiking boots and loose pants to keep the snake's fangs from reaching you. Hike with at least one other person. That person can get help if you are unable to hike out.

CAUTION

THERE MAY BE RATTLESNAKES IN THIS AREA.
RATTLESNAKES ARE ACTIVE AT NIGHT DURING THE
SUMMER. THEY WILL SEEK OUT SHADY PLACES DURING
THE HEAT OF THE DAY. CHILDREN SHOULD BE WARNED NOT
TO GO NEAR ANY SNAKE. REASONABLE WATCHFULNESS SHOULD
BE SUFFICIENT TO AVOID SNAKEBITE.

Right: Be aware of your surroundings when in rattlesnake territory.

Above: If you hear a rattlesnake's warning rattle, freeze. Find out where the snake is, then back up slowly and carefully. You both just want to get away from each other.

Do not attempt to pick up a rattlesnake. If you hear the rattler's warning as you are walking, but it hasn't bitten you yet, freeze. Find out where it is and if it is within striking distance. A rattler's striking distance can be up to half of its body length. Hold still until you've located the reptile. Wait for the snake to calm down and stop rattling. Slowly take small backward steps away from the reptile. If the snake begins to rattle again, stop, wait, and go again when the rattling has stopped. Go slowly—you both just want to get away from each other, but you want to do it safely.

What do you do if a rattlesnake bites? First, stay calm. The faster your heart beats, the faster the venom will spread. Identify the snake. Carefully note what it looks like—color, markings, head shape, etc. Get a picture if you can. The hospital needs to know what kind of snake bit you to give you the proper antivenin.

Although it is vital to get to a hospital as soon as possible, do not run. Allow others to carry you if they are able, but walk out if you must. Remove any jewelry before your body begins to swell up. Keep the wound below heart level. Wash out the wound with soap and water if it's available. Use a snakebite kit to suck out some of the venom. Do not try to suck out the venom with your mouth, and especially don't let a companion try it. This will put bacteria into the wound. Plus, any sore in a person's mouth would allow venom into that person.

Remember, as much as a 25 percent of the time, a rattlesnake does not inject venom into a bite. You may be one of the lucky ones. But it will take several precious minutes before you know for sure. Don't wait to find out. Get medical attention as soon as possible, and live to tell the story of being bitten by a rattlesnake.

Above: If you are bitten, there is a 25 percent chance that it is a dry bite, and the snake has not injected venom into you. Don't wait to find out for sure. Get to a hospital.

GLOSSARY

ANTIVENIN

Also called antivenom. This is a liquid used to treat and stop the effects of a bite from snakes, spiders, and other venomous creatures. Antivenin is created by injecting an animal, such as a horse or sheep, with a small amount of a specific creature's venom. The host animal produces antibodies against the venom, which can then be taken from the animal's blood and used to treat humans.

CLOTTING

The process in which a liquid, such as blood, dries and forms a thick mass. When a person receives a wound on their skin, under normal circumstances blood will lump together and form a scab over the area.

ENVENOMATE

To inject venom by biting or stinging. A venomous snake may bite a person without releasing its venom. This is called a "dry bite." Only when a snake injects venom into the bite wound is it said to envenomate a person.

HEMOTOXIN

A substance that destroys red blood cells. It keeps blood from clotting and causes tissue damage.

HERPETOLOGY

The study of reptiles (snakes, lizards, turtles, etc.) and amphibians (frogs, toads, salamanders, etc).

HYPODERMIC NEEDLE

A hollow needle used to inject fluid under the skin.

JACOBSON'S ORGAN

A sensory organ that snakes use to smell their prey.

LETHAL

Something that may cause death to a living thing.

NEUROTOXIN

A substance that causes damage or destroys nerves.

PEST

Any creature that there are too many of in a certain area. For example, because they reproduce so quickly and can cause damage to buildings and food supplies, mice and rats are often called pests.

SALIVA

A watery liquid found in the mouth.

SUCTION

To remove or draw away by using a sucking force. For example, venom may be suctioned out of a wound using a suction device that creates a vacuum and forces the fluid back up into the device.

TOXICOLOGIST

A person who studies the effects of poisons, and the treatment of poisoning, on living creatures.

INDEX

Right: Separated by glass, a boy gets a close-up view of a desert rattlesnake.